Suitcases and Backpacks

Growing through the Holocaust

CHAVA KOHAVI PINES

The publication of Suitcases and Backpacks in English was made possible with the kind help of the Guershoni Foundation.

Suitcases and Backpacks

Growing through the Holocaust

CHAVA KOHAVI PINES

English Translation by
Corinne Kohavi

Illustrated by
Juda Bakon

Suitcases and Backpacks

Growing through the Holocaust

Chava Kohavi Pines

Dekel Publishing House
www.dekelpublishing.com

North American rights by
Samuel Wachtman's Sons, Inc.
ISBN 978-1-888820-78-2

English translation: Corinne Kohavi
Language editing: Kathleen Roman
Illustrations: Juda Bakon

Cover design and typesetting by

For information contact:

Dekel Publishing House
P.O. Box 45094
Tel Aviv 6145002, Israel
Tel: +972 3506-3235
Fax: +972 3506-7332
Email: info@dekelpublishing.com

Samuel Wachtman's Sons, Inc.
2460 Garden Road, Suite C
Monterey, CA 93940, U.S.A.
Tel: 831 649-0669
Fax: 831 649-8007
Email: samuelwachtman@gmail.com

Table of Contents

Chapter 1:

Suitcases and Backpacks

The visits from the SA (men from the Sturmabteilung) demanding identity verification became more and more frequent.

The big suitcase used for trips overseas was sitting on a low table. It was always half full, mostly with things that we didn't need during a particular time of year, which was now autumn 1942.

The men in their brown uniforms came into our apartment again and again. They were accompanied by civilians who already knew too much about us. My stepfather got the documents showing he had the right to stay in Vienna with his family. As he was a young man during World War I he had fought on the German side. He had received awards and was handicapped during the war.

My mother filled bags and backpacks, which were sewn specifically for this purpose, and I tried hard to finish packing the suitcases.

My little sister went from one person to another, but no one had time for her.

It didn't make any sense to unpack all the bags, backpacks, and suitcases completely after the danger passed. They were always ready—for the next time.

Earlier they had come a few times only to get me. I had a different last name from everyone else in my family. After they cleared up any doubt they let me go.

But one time they actually took me with them.

They took me to a place I was very familiar with. It was the Jewish school on Sperlgasse Street where I had gone to school two years ago. At that time, it was one of the few schools where Jewish kids were still allowed to learn. Access to public schools for us Jews had been denied long ago.

Now there weren't any more tables or desks in the classrooms. Instead there were mattresses on the floor. People with little children sat on the mattresses or stood next to them. Others were trying to make their way through the room without stepping on someone.

Here I discovered a different world of grownups. Apparently, many didn't just leave their furniture and dishes at home, but their manners too.

I attracted attention and astonished smiles: a fourteen-year-old girl, all by herself, spreading out a yellow napkin in front of her just to avoid eating on the bare mattress.

Every day my mother came to the fence that cut off the entrance to the schoolyard. She brought me a well-packed pot of great food. She was not allowed to come in and only with help from the Jewish marshal was I able to get this warm package from home.

One day I was called to register in the schoolyard. There were tables that had once been used by the school teachers. But instead now they were used by the SA. The schoolyard was packed with a long line of Jews destined for deportation.

I arrived at the first table where my papers were reviewed. At the next table they were compared to a list—everything matched. After that, at the third table I received a cardboard sign with a number. A string was threaded through a small hole in the sign.

The next morning I would have to put the sign around my neck. They were planning to load us up on a truck and take us to the train station. At a specific gate a train was waiting to take us east.

That same evening, as I spread my dinner on the napkin, a marshal came. This time he informed me that I was free to go home.

My family was waiting for me at the fence.

But this had happened a year ago or even earlier.

Now we were already at the beginning of the fourth year of the war. There were more and more voided coupons on the food stamps that were given to us Jews to the point where we could barely buy anything anymore. We would use the few valuables that remained in our possession to buy some meat and lard on the black market.

The last Jewish school was closed long ago. We met in secret to learn in private homes that belonged to the students. But that didn't last very long either. My school friends disappeared one after another.

Some emigrated, others escaped, and the rest were deported.

The doorbell rang. Here they were again… But no, it was my friend Kurt.

When we strolled around the Jewish quarter, "decorated" with the yellow star, we often dreamed of the end of the war. The allies would of course win and we would still be in Vienna...

This time Kurt came to say goodbye. He and his family were scheduled to be transported on the next train. They were told they would be going to Theresienstadt, a concentration camp in Czechoslovakia.

I didn't know what the Theresienstadt Ghetto was in reality. There was talk, however, that the conditions were better there than in other ghettos. That's why it was intended for Jews who had special incomes.

I cried as I wondered whether we would ever see each other again.

One week later it was our turn. This time it was for real. We left our house.

Our Aryan neighbors were standing in the street. Their looks didn't reveal any concern.

The special train went to Czechoslovakia.

At a place called Bauschowitz, away from the train track, we came to a halt.

We were greeted by the SS (Schutzstaffel der NSDAP) who were accompanied by Czech army police and a few Jews wearing yellow armbands.

As they were loading the big suitcases on a carriage, the Jews with the yellow armbands told us with a strong Czech accent that the way from the train station to Theresienstadt was quite long.

I took as much of our luggage as I could carry and followed a group of people with my family toward the ghetto.

On the way, the carriage with our suitcases passed us. There were a few old people sitting on top. Instead of horses, the carriage was pulled and pushed by the men with yellow armbands.

Near the ghetto gate there was a big building, the Schleuse (Watergate). Here everything was carefully inspected and recorded. It was mostly Jews under SS control who were assigned to do the work.

I endured the first disinfection of my life. I couldn't really understand why they inspected the seam of my coat until someone explained to me that some people sewed gold and silver into their clothing.

In the meantime others were going through the backpacks and bags that I had carried with great effort all this way. They were looking for anything valuable and whatever they found was confiscated.

Finally, with my backpack on and a bag in each hand, I left the Schleuse with my family. We never saw our big suitcases again. They stayed there, as was the case for everyone. The Schleuse didn't let them pass.

I was only able to walk slowly with the crowd. We were watched with curious eyes by the "old" ghetto occupants who had arrived earlier and were lined up on both sides of the road. My eyes wandered from one to another. I was looking for anyone I might know.

Suddenly I saw him.

"Kurt!" I yelled, putting the bags down and running toward him. I hugged him and kissed him—in front of everyone.

Afterward I quickly picked up the bags and hurried to catch up with my family.

There on the sidewalk stood a sixteen-year-old boy who was completely embarrassed.

I had found my friend.

Chapter 2:
Marzipan

Marzipan—a white substance made with almonds and sugar. The word alone made my mouth water. But that wasn't more than a memory.

It was 1943.

A small group of girls and boys in the Theresienstadt Ghetto tried to solve a big problem: How should we celebrate Willi's birthday?

Willi, a tall and heavier-set boy, was about to turn sixteen years old.

A small note was passed around from hand to hand: “Monday at six...here.”

At six o’clock in the evening Willi visited his parents as was the custom with most of us. We didn’t live with our parents. All the boys in our group were put in a room in the living quarters of L214, and the girls were put in L414.

“Here” was the boys’ room with the plain three-level bunk beds found in the ghettos. Alongside the bottom bed was a board that served as a bench, and together with a table it formed a seating area. This was the place where we got together for our meeting.

That Sunday we told our parents that tomorrow we would be coming a bit later than usual.

The discussion began with the presentation of the following problem: “Tell me, what should we do?”

Silence all around.

Then someone suggested that everyone should give some of their sugar ration for Willi. Maybe we’d even add some margarine.

“Pretty good, but not much of a party,” someone said out loud.

“He should get a cake,” I whispered.

Someone nearby heard me and said as if speaking to himself, “A cake...a birthday cake...”

Again everyone was quiet. Memories arose.

There were once birthdays, when we still lived at home—children, like all other children.

A white tablecloth covered the table. In the middle was a cake covered with chocolate frosting and decorated with small candles. One candle for every year and an additional one to grow on.

Was it really that long ago?

"Maybe we'll get Willi a whole buchtel and share the leftovers?"

This suggestion brought us back into reality. A buchtel was a square-shaped sweet roll made with yeast dough that was served once a week for lunch with caramel sauce. When it was served fresh the people in the ghetto savored it like a special delicacy.

"But unfortunately there won't be any buchteln served on his birthday!"

That was a serious counterargument because old buchteln turned as hard as a rock.

"Maybe we can do something anyway. I'm ready to try," I suggested.

We started a community collection and we saved enough for two buchteln, some sugar, margarine, and marmalade.

Willi didn't know anything about it. He would continue to get his entire meal rations and the "supplies" were well hidden.

The night before his birthday I started working on it. With the help of a hammer I crumbled up the hardened buchteln. Adding water, sugar, and margarine turned them into dough from which I formed some small fruit: pears, apples, cherries, and strawberries. I basted them partially with red marmalade and placed a small leaf in each one.

Wasn't this like real marzipan fruit?

Willi found the plate on his bed. He could hardly contain himself.

But boys don't cry…

Chapter 3:

Hanukkah Lights

The end of 1943.

Outside a war was raging, and we had been locked up in the Theresienstadt Ghetto for over a year.

It was getting close to Hanukkah for the second time. Last year we still had candles from back home, but since then they had become a rare commodity. It was very clear that this time there weren't going to be any Hanukkah lights. Therefore, we wouldn't be singing nor would we be playing with the dreidel. In short, we wouldn't be celebrating Hanukkah this year.

But our youth group wasn't going to settle for that.

A few days before Hanukkah I entered the room of my group in L214 and noticed immediately that something didn't seem right.

My eyes wandered from one person to the other—everyone was silent.

"What happened?" I asked, worried. "You're holding something back from me. Is someone sick?"

"No," began the first one hesitantly. "I picked up some wood from the construction site, for the Hanukkah menorah."

"We also have paint," added the second one.

"Even electric wires aren't a problem," added another.

All of a sudden I felt that all the eyes were directed toward me.

"What do you want from me?" I asked, surprised.

"Come with me and I will explain it to you," said Emanuel, the watchmaker, and pulled me out of the house.

Once we got away a bit he whispered, "We have almost everything for an electric Hanukkah menorah. Only the lights are missing and you are the only one who can get them for us."

With growing astonishment I asked, "Really, me? Electric lights? Where would I get them?"

"From the church," he answered.

In the middle of the ghetto there was a church. At the top of the steeple was a clock. If anyone still possessed such a thing and hadn't exchanged it for food, he would set his watch according to the steeple. Emanuel's honorary job was to climb up the tower daily to wind up the clock.

"I found two boxes of electric lights at the church. They were probably used for Christmas decorations," he said. "You can hide them under your long coat and no one will notice."

We arrived at the church. Emanuel opened the small side door as usual and entered the church. After I briefly checked around me, I snuck in too, and he locked the door carefully behind us.

Then he approached an old chest of drawers and pulled out two long boxes. I hid them under my coat—they almost reached the hem.

Emanuel climbed up the tower stairs to set the clock. I had to wait until he came back down. Only a few minutes passed, but to me it seemed like hours. Maybe someone had seen me after all and would report me to the German command post?

There was an oppressive semi-darkness in the church.

Just let's get out of here, I thought.

Finally Emanuel reappeared next to me and pulled me out of the church.

I breathed a sigh of relief.

But the most difficult part of this undertaking still lay ahead. In order to get back to the boys' living quarters at L214, I had to walk across the German Street. SS and spies would come by. The street led directly to the ghetto's main command post.

The Jewish ghetto guard kept watch there. As soon as a German drew near, all passengers were stopped until the street was clear again.

What if one of the Germans passing by noticed by chance my coat that was puffed out on the side, my arms that clung against my body to assist my hands that were buried deep in my coat pockets to protect the boxes? And what if he called me over and ordered me to open my coat and the lights were revealed?

It was very clear to me that my and my parents' destiny would be definitively decided.

As we approached the barrier I could only hear the beat of my heart that seemed like it was about to burst.

It seemed to me that the passers-by would look at me carefully. But it was probably just my imagination. Nobody seemed to care, even when I crossed the street by myself.

I got back to L214 in one piece.

During the week of Hanukkah we locked the door to the room every night and put covers over the windows so that no outsider could detect our unusual menorah. Every day we changed the colors of the candles. On the last evening the menorah glowed with exclusively blue and white candles.

We sat around the table and had just started to sing, when all of a sudden someone knocked on the door.

The singing stopped. We looked at each other and turned pale. Somebody pulled the plug out of the outlet and the room became completely dark.

The first one to feel courage asked, "Who's there?"

The voice of the warden answered and a sigh of relief came over us.

The key turned in the lock, the Hanukkah menorah glowed once again with its electric lights, and the singing started once more.

Chapter 4:

Applause

Once again I didn't get a ticket to the concert.

An usher stood at the entrance. But for me, as it was for other teenagers in the ghetto, he wasn't an obstacle. I just waited until he got really busy with checking tickets and then snuck behind him into the hall.

I leaned against the wall in the back full of excitement. There was a big black wing with an open lid on stage and a stool in front of it.

It became quiet in the hall.

I discovered an empty seat.

The gray-haired pianist bowed before us and briefly announced the program. Then he sat down at the piano. The felt-covered wooden hammers hit the strings and you could hear a few notes. One note after another, like beads on a string, emerged from the piano.

The melody filled the room.

Loud applause followed, thanking the artist.

Then there was a short break.

The guy sitting next to me, a boy around my age, started talking to me in Czech. "I don't speak Czech," I answered, and that was the only full sentence I knew in that language.

After he introduced himself in German he asked me why I wasn't applauding. My short answer was that we didn't applaud in the youth movement.

Afterward we talked about music. I told him that I would like to continue taking violin lessons. I had found a blind man who offered to give me lessons for a piece of sugar and margarine.

That's when Rolf, my neighbor, interrupted me and told me that he had a friend who played the violin. They lived in the same house—surely he would be willing to give me free violin lessons.

The break was over. The hall transformed itself once again into an island that was separated from the ghetto by an ocean of sound.

At the end there was clapping and shouting until the audience received an encore. I also didn't applaud at that time and Rolf did the same out of politeness. On the way home we decided to meet at Rolf's house. There he would introduce me to the young musician—my new teacher.

Already the next day I went to the house that he had described to me and climbed up to the attic.

I was facing a row of doors. Electricians lived here and Rolf was one of them. These houses were called Bungalows—a kind of barrack made out of wooden boards. There weren't any walls between men and women as was the custom in the rest of the ghetto, and the families lived together.

Rolf was waiting for me in front of the door.

There were a few sweets sitting on the table and his mom invited me to take some. Yes, that's right, you serve a guest—I had almost forgotten that.

Only when I reminded Rolf did he go to get the teacher. Tommy, the "teacher," was a tall, broad-shouldered boy whose baby face alone revealed his age. He was allowed to live here because his father worked for the electric company as an engineer.

After a short conversation we set a date for the first violin lesson. Tommy planned to come to L414 at a time when we wouldn't bother the girls in my room too much.

The whole deal almost fell through when I offered to pay. He sternly refused and I gave up trying.

Tommy took the lessons very seriously. He was both a teacher and a friend to me.

I didn't meet with Rolf anymore.

Preparations were going on in the ghetto: A library was about to be opened, the kids were invited to a playground, colorful signs were everywhere, and in the center a park started to turn green. All this and much more was planned for the visit of the delegation of the international Red Cross.

At that time an orchestra was put together. There were plenty of artists of all sorts in Theresienstadt and the best musicians were picked for the event.

The concerts will be held in a pavilion. The audience would be sitting on folding chairs in the afternoon sun to listen to the musician—an idyllic picture for the Red Cross.

One time Tommy accompanied me to one of the orchestra rehearsals.

Inside a remote house, where one needed to get a special ID to get in, sat musicians of every age. The conductor made them repeat the same measures countless times.

There was a special atmosphere in the neglected hall. The people gathered there were only interested in the pure sounds of the notes and the perfection of the rhythm. The hardship of the life in the ghettos seemed to have been banished here.

The day of the first concert had arrived. I sat on one of the chairs in front of the pavilion hours before it started. Out of fear that someone would take my seat I didn't move from my spot. As time went on the seats around me filled up.

Most of the people attending were older and talked about other concerts they had heard, other conductors and musicians they had known—"there," "long ago"—in a whole world that had existed before I was born or during my early childhood.

The musicians in the pavilion sat down. Tommy sat down in the first row, very close to the audience.

Exactly at a predetermined time the conductor climbed up the few steps, bowed, and lifted his baton.

As if with a magic wand he transformed the ghetto into a Karlsbad or Marienbad where all pains were healed.

The audience sat there looking pleased. But as the concert came to an end and the illusion disappeared. At first there was silence and then continuous applause.

Even I clapped my hands—evidently I had forgotten the Youth Movement.

Chapter 5:

The Ring

We worked in two shifts in the Central Dental Clinic: the first one in the morning, the second one in the afternoon. Even though I wasn't working on my own, my friends decided that the birthday present for Shalom was my job.

Shalom was our youth leader. He was tall, handsome, and had a nice demeanor. His intelligence was far above average and he had an amazing memory.

Late at night, after the lights went off in youth dormitory L214, he went to the empty secretary office loaded with books; he remained there until early in the morning. We really admired his will to overcome fatigue and hunger.

All of that earned him favor and endless admiration amongst us.

Now his nineteenth birthday was right around the corner.

After a few meetings we decided that we would give him a ring—to be exact, a signet ring.

We didn't have any means to buy a ring. My friends were under the impression that pouring a finger ring was similar to pouring a crown for a tooth. That's why this job was assigned to me.

But what should I use to pour the ring? There was no chance that we would be able to get ahold of some gold.

If not gold, then silver would do!

Luckily one of us received a silver spoon for this purpose from his parents.

At the time our group was also busy with something else. In my friend's room there was a sort of a community checkout where we would store a portion of our food ration. You could find some bread, sugar, margarine, and similar treasures in a small homemade wooden cabinet. These were mainly saved for Friday evening as a special something extra in honor of Shabbat.

It wasn't easy at all to save a portion of the food ration as we were never full anyway.

We didn't tell our parents—they didn't approve at all of the community ideas regarding meals.

All of a sudden we discovered that our reserves, without us having using them, had diminished.

We discussed it with Shalom. Nobody thought it was one of us. Only Shalom suggested Ruben.

Ruben was older than we were, about as old as Shalom, and lived together with his younger brother who belonged to our group. He was tall and skinny with a bit of a hunched back, and he was always hungry. Of course he wasn't present during this discussion.

As Shalom made this suggestion, the younger brother shut his eyes and we all were quiet and ashamed.

We decided to wait for the thief. Said and done, but no one had been caught.

My afternoon shift began.

Toward the end of the day things slowed down at the dental clinic and that's when it was easier to work on something personal.

I formed a pink wax ring around a finger stump made out of plaster. Now the work came to a point where I had to include someone in the secret.

The technician, my boss, was a kind and people-loving man. One time he noticed during the early shift that I wasn't eating. He asked, concerned, if I wasn't feeling well, and I admitted to him my habit of eating my bread ration for the entire day on the evening before. That was the only way I was able to stop the hunger pains.

The next morning he brought an extra sandwich just for me. Thereafter, he did so every day—for the rest of the entire week.

Now I explained to him the thing with the ring and he understood.

The guys in our group were gloomy. Especially as things were being stolen next door as well. That's where the older boys like Shalom lived, who sometimes received food packages from outside.

One day, after everyone had left the room, Moshe—one of the older boys—looked through his friends' beds and other things. He found some breadcrumbs that had come from his own package in Shalom's bed.

Moshe only told the secret to people from our group. No one but them knew about it.

One morning, after everyone left to go to work, they both returned secretly to the room, climbed up to the third level of the wooden bunk beds, and remained lying there, quiet and still.

Shalom entered the room, but only to walk through it to get to his room.

Finally everything was ready for the pouring of the ring.

I carefully washed the pink wax out of the cast with hot water. Then I broke the silver spoon into small pieces, turned on the burner, and waited until the metal turned into a reddish-yellow liquid. A few quick movements through the air, and the glowing silver disappeared into the cast.

Impatiently I waited for the results—was it a success? Maybe I would have to start all over?

As I broke the cast into little pieces, the ring appeared. As I had hoped, the metal had filled the entire space.

I still had to do a lot of grinding down and sanding and to try it out at the end, but the main part of the work was complete.

After a short time Shalom's initials decorated the signet ring.

It happened only after a third attempt. Holding their breath, they waited until Shalom opened the supply cabinet and stood there with margarine, sugar, and bread in his hands, ready to leave the room. At that moment the two boys surprised him.

When I came back to L214 that same day I found out what had happened.

At first I could hardly believe it: How was it possible—our Shalom?! Then I felt hurt. The person we had trusted cheated his students and friends and stole their bread right from their mouths.

He was a weakling.

Our group was depressed.

Shalom was cast out of the circle of the He'Halutz youth movement. Afterward none of us spoke so much as a word with him.

We tossed the silver ring into the gutter.

Chapter 6:

One Kilo of Chocolate

The central post office was located on the ground floor of L414; there were a lot of people coming and going. Even though the children's home was in the same building, I had never been to the post office. This was where people from Czechoslovakia received presents from their relatives outside the ghetto. None of the children in our home was that lucky.

We watched them carrying their treasures through the courtyard from a window in the hallway. In our fantasy the contents of these packages was very clear to us; for example, a lightly browned mixture made out of flour, fat, and sugar, which filled up a big tin can. With the help of a knife you could take a small layer and spread it on a piece of bread.

Once I had a little bite of it.

One day Ruth—a girlfriend who worked at the post office—turned to me and told me a secret. There was a package with my name on it.

Apparently she could see my disbelief and quickly added that even though the package had my name on it, it wasn't meant for me.

I knew that nobody would have sent me a package, but I was hoping...maybe...?

Ruth continued with her explanation. She knew the girl who this package was for. However, she wasn't in the ghetto any longer, as she had been deported eastward. The package had been at the post office for many weeks.

Ruth placed a note in my hands. I should simply go to the post office and tell them that I was expecting a package; she had written down the details for me.

The next day I followed her advice and picked up the package at the post office.

Without opening it I went straight to my mother. I placed the package on her bed and explained how I had received it.

There was great excitement. What could be in it?

Finally I untied the string and removed the wrapping paper.

As I opened the lid, something appeared, something far beyond my imagination. On pink paper, one row next to another, there was brown and already a bit grayish-looking chocolate…one kilo of chocolate.

After the initial surprise we had to decide what to do with it. Should we just eat the chocolate slowly? The thought alone made my mouth water.

My mother left it up to me to decide.

No. Everyone should try just a little piece to refresh their memory. The rest we should keep stored away in case the little food we received in the ghetto was completely eliminated.

My mother hid the chocolate according to my wishes in a safe place.

Time passed, and my awareness that there was a kilo of chocolate waiting for me remained only in my subconsciousness.

In October of 1944 we were called to be transported.

We went to get the chocolate out of its secret place. My mother put it in her big purse from which she wouldn't be separated—that's what she said.

Late in the afternoon, we were told to get into the wagons. We had our hands full with bags and the SS hurried us along with their rifles.

It was a passenger car, but it was already halfway loaded with bags, backpacks, and suitcases. We were to find a place to sit on top of these mountains.

More and more people were pushed into the train cars.

"Seventy-five!" yelled one of the SS, and he threw the door shut with a bang.

The windows were locked.

Hours passed, it became dark, and the train still sat at the station in the ghetto.

From time to time they came to check on us. Flashlights were pointed toward us—counting once again, "Seventy-five!" "Everything is alright!" Again the doors were shut with a loud bang, and seventy-five Jews of all ages remained half sitting, half leaning back against their luggage.

Finally all the train cars were locked up. A sharp whistle blew and the train started moving.

Where to?

A sleepless night. In the morning we ate from our supplies and drank from the thermos. We didn't touch the chocolate; we thought it hadn't come to that point yet.

Every now and then someone commented about our destination.

By the afternoon I had become really uncomfortable sitting down. Every movement of my legs—buried under backpacks and bags—would cause the piles of luggage to collapse. That's why I tried not to move them for as long as possible.

The second night the air was suffocating.

A long night, full of moaning and crying.

In the morning we arrived in an unusual place; there were fences with barbed wire, as far as the eye could see, and watchtowers!

"We are in Auschwitz," said someone inside the wagon. This name didn't mean anything to me.

Many hours of the train cars moving from one gate to another.

Big barracks appeared between the fences, but no people. All of a sudden we saw a group of people dressed in prison uniforms and a man hitting them with a whip.

Instinctively I was overcome with immense fear.

It was noon by the time the car doors were finally opened with a shout: "Get out! Quickly! Leave everything behind in the train!"

My mother opened her purse; there it was, the chocolate. As fast as we could we stuffed the squares into our pockets. We had put on many layers of clothing in preparation for the transport so we had a lot of pockets.

Once outside the train car, it was a beautiful sunny autumn day.

My mother and I were holding hands, and we slowly moved with the mass of people toward the end of the gate.

All of a sudden we stood in front of a broad-shouldered man wearing a leather coat. He didn't say anything, just pointed with his thumb, over here, over there, and we were forced apart from each other.

Shortly thereafter I marched with a group of girls toward the shower rooms under the supervision of the SS. I had to leave all of my clothes behind there, including the pockets full of chocolate.

I remained naked and shaved clean.

Chapter 7:

The Headscarf

It was morning; grey dawn was spreading. Slowly but surely my environment was becoming dimmer—the three-level wooden beds, and rows of shaved heads that were ordered to face the feeding trough in the middle of the barracks. Morning was something without hope in Auschwitz.

I didn't get out of bed, as I was to remain in bed until I was ordered to do something else.

I didn't get dressed, as the only thing I still had in my possession was my nightgown and my underwear, which remained on me like my skin.

I didn't wash myself and I didn't go to the bathroom. We were only allowed to do so when we received a command. Only then were we allowed to go, under the watch of the capo, to the latrine or to the water fountain.

I stayed in bed, staring into space, and I made it a habit not to think.

The door opened and a sunbeam entered the barracks. All heads looked up from the beds at the same time.

Two women came by my block with a covered stretcher. The cover moved a bit—there was a bluish-looking foot. Whispers went through the beds from one level to the next throughout the barracks: "She went to the barbed wire…"

Someone next to me noticed that there were only nine of us in the block.

The tenth!

Ruja…

Had it been yesterday or the day before? It was difficult here to distinguish one day from the next. In any case, that morning the capo from our block, a heavyset woman who didn't have to suffer from starvation, brought a bag.

"Here, take some!" she said and put it in the feeding trough.

Colorful rags peeked from the bag.

Quickly the picture in our barrack changed. Girls stormed from every direction toward the bag and soon they looked like a pile of heads and hands. There was cussing in many different languages as each tried to rip the bag out of one another's hands.

I also wanted to get to the bag—for only a pitiful rag I could use to cover my bald head! If I could only look like a girl again, not like a monkey. But as I finally reached the bag, it was already empty. Only two girls were left fighting for the same rag, one pulled one way and the other pulled the opposite way. The material wasn't strong enough. The one who ended up with the bigger piece quickly went to her bed.

I followed her. She sat there and was clinging to her prize: a piece of red material with white dots. Then she wrapped it around her head, and nine girls full of jealousy observed her every move.

It was Ruja from our "group of ten"; a beautiful girl—even without hair.

Slowly everything calmed down; the usual daily muttering and whispering returned to the barracks.

That day it was my turn to pick up the food.

I stood with the others at the barracks entrance in front of the capo's private room on the block and grabbed the handle of a big empty milk jug. Ruja, who had decorated her head with the scarf, held on tightly to the other side. The troop took off in pairs with the capo.

Outside, a gloomy, rainy day. Poland in the middle of October.

Big barracks in endless rows.

On the horizon there was smoke rising toward the grey sky—the crematorium.

In the morning they led us to the showers, to "disinfect." I stood there waiting for hours all lathered up with soap until it was my turn to rinse off.

When I finally got out of the showers, it had already gotten dark outside. Flames illuminated the night sky, rising with the smoke from the crematorium. In only a nightgown and a pair of underwear I stood trembling in the coolness of the night.

All of a sudden a thought crossed my mind: *Now, just now my mother is being burned!*

But now I wasn't thinking about that any more when I saw the crematorium.

The capo led us to the place where they gave out the food. The jugs were filled with soup, and in the meantime the capo was busy in the kitchen with private supply affairs. We stood outside and waited. The barracks on the right is the quarantine, someone told us; this is where they would bring the sick. But it was better if you never came here—it could be the way to the crematorium.

A man in striped prison clothes approached us. On his left near the shoulders, next to his number, was a green triangle. The sign of a criminal. He could move around freely here. He was neither Jew nor political opponent...only a murderer or similar criminal.

Apparently Ruja caught his attention because he turned toward her.

I can only remember one sentence: "For a piece of bread or a cigarette," he said, "I can get any woman in the camp."

The capo returned from the kitchen, and our small troop marched on toward the barracks.

It was raining. The full jugs were heavy. The wooden Dutch clogs sank deep into the mud. Every step while wearing them was difficult, and on top of that they were too big on me.

It was a long way; the electric barbed wire accompanied us everywhere. I was only a few steps away from the fence. Again and again I let go of the handle, and Ruja had to wait until I was able to pull my shoe out of the mud. The capo noticed and urged me along.

One thing I knew: I couldn't leave the jug on the side of the road. We had to bring it to the barracks...no matter what.

Finally the jug reached its destination.

Very weak, I returned to my spot on the third level of bunk beds. All of a sudden my bed became my refuge—that's where I wanted to stay and never leave again.

I lay at the edge of the bed, an unfortunate spot at night time. The only blanket we had for the ten of us never reached all the way to the ones sleeping on the edges.

Ruja lay at the other edge of the bed. From here it was easier to get out of bed at night without stepping on others who were sleeping.

Did Ruja secretly escape out of the barracks that night? I will never find out.

And why did she touch the barbed wire? What was she trying to find there—was it herself that she had lost?

But I wasn't thinking about that.

I just saw a bluish foot—her headscarf was covered up with the blanket.

Chapter 8:

The Scream

They were thrown toward me, one by one from a big pile of clothes—underwear, a blouse, a skirt, and a long coat. As I didn't have a bath towel to dry off with, I put them on my wet body.

Lined up in rows of three, we marched out of the showers.

It was noon and I was at a train station once more.

In the morning I was trembling in the cold at the roll call. It was the end of October in Poland and I was only wearing a pair of underwear and a nightgown.

All of a sudden they called my name, but I wasn't the only one who stepped out from the row. We were sent to work, we were told. My heart was full of awful worries. Anything unusual from the daily routine could mean death.

Earlier that morning a Jewish female doctor came by the barracks; of course she was also a prisoner. We had to line up and one after the other step up to her.

She sat on a stool and she felt around each woman's abdomen. When she became suspicious, she asked the fateful question, "Are you pregnant?"

The answer was always, "No." Even the doctor knew that ahead of time. A pregnant woman only had to await one thing—death.

Now after the showers we assumed that we were being taken out of the camp.

A capo approached us and whispered, "You are lucky. You are being taken to a good place."

In the afternoon the train cars arrived at the gate; this time they were cattle cars. On the very top there was a small opening to let some air in for the cows that were taken to be slaughtered. But even they were enforced with cross bars and barbed wire.

As we got into the train car we received our daily bread ration. We ate standing because there wasn't enough room to sit down.

The doors were locked from the outside, but the train didn't leave Auschwitz until it was pitch dark.

We traveled all night long, leaning against one another.

At the first signs of dawn we took turns looking out of the opening. We were driving through a rural area, but nobody knew where we were.

Finally the train stopped at a station and someone was able to read the sign: Merzdorf.

There were a few SS women at the gate. The doors were opened and after they had us line up in rows of three we began to move, accompanied by the SS.

As a group of women with shaved heads and rags for clothes, we were marched through a village followed by half-astonished and half-careless looks.

Not far from the village there were a few grey buildings surrounding a courtyard. On the first and second story of the main building were the many departments of the spinning mill. The third floor already housed some women that had been brought in from the Lodz Ghetto. The female doctor's room was also located there.

We were being put on the top floor. A nice surprise was awaiting us. No longer did we have just *one* bed and *one* blanket for ten women, where one could only lay on one's side and never be covered well. Now the wooden beds were for two and there was a blanket for every woman.

On top of that, they gave each of us a triangular, grey piece of cloth to cover our bald heads.

The camp filled up in no time. There were three hundred of us on the top floor.

They divided us up into groups for each department in the factory. I was working in the fine spinning department. All day long we walked alongside the machines to join together the endless tearing threads. Mercy for the one who was caught standing still when only one of the threads on the machine was torn!

The workday ended with a roll call in the courtyard. Afterward we had to stand in line to get soup and bread. With the food in our hands we went to the top floor and the door was locked from the outside; after a while the lights were turned off as well. After a fourteen-hour work day the little "pets," which found their permanent home in our beds and clothes, really didn't bother me in my sleep.

All the groups of women from the camp except the one that they called "transport" worked in the main building. They had to transport the raw material from the warehouse to the main building. Every day they loaded the firmly compressed flax bales on the wagon. During the winter, from what was then East Germany, in the cold, snow, rain, and mud these women pushed and pulled the wagon. Horses had long ago been sent off for use in the war.

In the adjacent bed, one level below me, two sisters who worked with the transport group slept. They had also come to Auschwitz from Theresienstadt.

When I opened my eyes in the morning, I found them already dressed in their coats ready for the departure.

Every evening a new debate between the sisters started. They spoke quietly in Czech, a language I only knew little of; nevertheless I understood that the younger one didn't want to accept any portion of her sister's ration. In the end the younger one always gave up and ate. Afterward they waited, still with their coats on, until the lights went out, and only then did they climb up into their beds.

As the months went on it became clear. I picked it up from the whispers all around me. The little sister was pregnant. A terrible secret. When the female SS commander found out about it and told her superior, the woman would be sent to her death.

But the big coat, the other women from the transport group, and most of all her sister helped make sure that time went by and nothing like that happened.

One night at the end of the winter I woke up—the light was on.

I heard a few solitary voices that soon turned into a turmoil. "She is in labor!" they yelled, and, "She needs the doctor!" The door was still locked! Two hundred ninety-nine women were frantically walking back and forth, and one woman was near her end.

All of a sudden someone opened the window and a loud yell came from everywhere: "Doctor! Doctor!"

After a while, which seemed like an eternity, the door was unlocked and the female doctor appeared with a female SS matron. The pregnant woman and her sister went down with them to the third floor.

Afterward the lights were turned off again and each of us remained in the dark with our thoughts.

The next morning it was announced that she had had a son.

The war was near its end. The connection between pregnancy and death was stopped.

Even in the hearts of the SS women—all unmarried—a spark of humanity awoke. They put the mother and her baby in the showers on the third floor, which we weren't allowed to use.

The following Sunday after the roll call they permitted us to take a peek at the newborn.

I was looking at him and thinking, *such a tiny being who came to us as if from another world. I wonder if he'll survive?*

There were children who had a fairy godmother standing over their beds when they were born.

I heard that the child survived. His father also returned from the concentration camp and they now live together in a foreign country.

Chapter 9:

Forest Magic

Many songs have been written to praise the beautiful month of May.

But I hardly knew its magic. For the past seven years, since my childhood, my world had become so restricted that there was no room left for spring. First I moved to a special quarter in Vienna that was meant for Jews; later I was put behind walls in the Theresienstadt Ghetto; and finally, via Auschwitz, I ended up in a spinning mill near Breslau.

In the beginning of May 1945, this factory was my world.

One beautiful morning, four hundred women and girls assembled in the courtyard for the roll call when all of a sudden a siren went off.

"Alarm!" yelled the female SS overseers, turning toward us. "We are going into the bomb shelter. There is no room for you. Stay nearby and as soon as you hear the sirens again return immediately to the factory!"

Within just a few moments the courtyard emptied. The Germans were hiding in the basements and we "prisoners" scattered all around.

Recognizing an opportunity, I found myself with two other girls crossing a small creek near the factory.

Even though we had been here for over half a year, we didn't know the area. We had never left the factory courtyard. Yet if someone was watching us that morning, they would have had to assume we knew every tree and bush.

We didn't exchange one word.

We were headed toward a wooded hill. We didn't see anyone—everyone was in the bomb shelters.

Finally we got to the woods; our feet touched soft moss. I bent over to touch it with my hands—it was wet and had a distinct odor. The sun flickered through the tree branches and painted an endless picture of different shapes of shadows and light spots. Birds were sitting on branches in the trees, their voices filing the woods.

None of us three knew what was happening. It was like a fairytale and miracles all around us. After we had been deprived of nature for seven years, the forest captivated us with all its magic.

We weren't just walking anymore, but skipping and turning around in circles. We rejoiced and moved forward in a weird kind of dance.

The path led us, as we really didn't have a specific destination in mind. We just wanted to get farther and farther away, without anyone stopping us—no police, no fences, just like free human beings.

It felt like many hours had passed when the trees began to thin at the other end of the forest. There was a village right in front of us.

Where were we?

Only when we approached one of the houses did we learn that it was a neighboring village.

One of the female farmers let us in. We sat on a wooden bench and heard a voice from the radio:

"Today, on the eighth day of May, 1945, Germany surrendered to the allies…"

Chapter 10:

A Russian Soldier

Again I was on a train.

This time it was a train without a guard, and nobody was waiting, not even the SS. They had already taken off their uniforms a few weeks ago and hoped no one would recognize them. Maybe some of them even sat in the wagon with me—who knows?

A few hours ago near the Czech boarder I said goodbye to my two girlfriends. One of them went to Prague, the other to Pressburg. Both of them invited me to go with them. But I wanted to return to Vienna. I was hoping…

In Auschwitz my mother went in the direction from which there was no return. But maybe my father was still alive.

So I continued on my journey by myself.

The refugee train moved very slowly.

There were a lot of Germans from all over the country sitting around me very closely who wanted to return "home" to their motherland. This time they left everything behind.

It was already evening as the news spread in the train: the train tracks had been destroyed, probably by a bomb from the allies. We couldn't go any further. We had to walk this section of the way, and we could possibly find a train on the other side.

I got off with my suitcase in my hand.

It was still daylight as I passed by a small village.

The suitcase, which I had received from a farmer near the work camp, continued to get heavier. It only contained a few clothes that had been given to me, but my strength was running out fast. The distance between me and the other travelers increased.

At the last sign of dusk a Russian soldier pushing a bicycle passed me.

Russian soldiers had freed us from the work camp. They had brought cows and slaughtered them to feed the hungry women. Some died from the fullness.

So why shouldn't I turn toward a Russian soldier and ask him for a favor?

With a little Czech and a few gestures I explained to him my request until he understood to load my suitcase on the back of his bicycle.

I walked alongside.

We had left the village long behind us and it was already completely dark when he all of a sudden turned toward a tunnel, which led under the railway.

I tried to explain to him that I needed to continue alongside the tracks, but he wasn't even listening.

He left his bicycle in the tunnel and hugged me and pressed me against the wall.

I screamed, but there was nobody except him to hear me. I fought against him with all my strength. I tried to explain to him that I had come from the concentration camp and I said simple words in Czech like "no mother," "no father," "Nazis"—and hoped that he would understand them.

Then he shined a flashlight in my face; he pointed his revolver against my chest.

With tears in my eyes I shouted that he should just shoot me. I didn't have a living soul any longer anyway.

Maybe he understood. But it was more probable that my short hair and my pitiful appearance as a camp survivor did the trick.

Angrily he threw the suitcase from his bicycle and quickly left.

I picked up the suitcase and left the tunnel with my whole body shaking.

So I wouldn't get lost in the dark I got up to the train tracks and walked beside them. Not far off I saw some lights. That was the next train station.

As I reached the small waiting room I found the floor was already taken up by people; they prepared to spend the night here.

Just as I found a place to sit, my neighbor, a Russian soldier, offered me a piece of a sugar cube and some vodka with a smile.

I answered with a fake calmness: "No thanks," and got up as fast as I could.

The soldier looked at me astonished: What had he done to me?

I was looking for a place on the opposite side of the hall. I sat there the whole night and waited for dawn.

They promised us a train in the morning.

Chapter 11:

Still on the Way

It had been an hour since the train stopped. We could see greening fields through the windows. The people in the train car began to guess what could be growing in the fields.

Two young boys sitting across from me went out into the field. Other people from the wagons followed them. Shortly thereafter they returned with their arms loaded with onions. They offered them to everyone sitting nearby.

I took a few onions and ate the long green stalks. There was nothing to tone down the taste—there wasn't any bread or any other food left over.

After the onion meal I got involved in a conversation with the two boys. When they heard that I had come from the concentration camp, they told me that they had been imprisoned as communists. I didn't argue their point. It was nice to chat.

In the meantime the train headed toward Vienna.

At the next train station the situation became desperate—there weren't even any green onion fields.

The boys suggested that I leave the train with them. It would be better to continue on foot and beg for food from the villagers than to starve to death here. That sounded reasonable, and I followed them.

Shortly thereafter we reached the first houses.

We stood in front of a locked gate leading to a farm.

When we rang the doorbell we only heard dogs barking.

The boys knocked on the door with their fists and I yelled as loudly as I could, "Is anyone home?"

After a long wait and additional ringing of the doorbell the gate opened. A woman with a headscarf and an obviously scared expression stood in front of us.

"What do you want?" she asked.

We begged for food.

"The Russians didn't leave much," she said, but she could give us a couple of cooked potatoes. She brought them into the courtyard and as we were eating she told us about the Russians. They raped the women and shaved their hair and loaded all the cattle onto their trucks. There weren't any men there to protect them. They hadn't returned from the war, she said.

She didn't talk about the Nazis who were hiding.

We continued on our way and in each courtyard we only found women and children and heard more or less the same stories.

We spent the night in an abandoned house.

In the morning we marched on a country road toward Vienna.

The boys bent down often to pick up cigarette butts. They had probably been thrown out by passing troops.

It didn't take very long until my eyes were able to spot the white remains on the grey country road.

In the next village we happened to come across a military truck. A Russian soldier loaded up some potatoes with a pitchfork. From time to time his friend who had been resting took a turn.

My traveling companions had an idea. They were willing to help load if in return they could hitch a ride in the truck to Vienna.

With my broken Czech and various gestures I explained the offer to the Russians. They immediately agreed and brought another pitchfork. Thereafter, they watched the loading from off to one side.

After the work was completed the boys climbed up on the truck and sat on top of the potato mountain; I received a seat in the cabin.

On the way it started to rain.

Vague outlines of the church towers of Vienna started to appear on the horizon. The city seemed to me both familiar and foreign at the same time. Had I really only been gone for three years?

Chapter 12:

The Door

Again I stood in front of the door, a long journey behind me.

Everything had changed; only the hallway and the doors remained in the same spot.

This was our door, the entry to our apartment. It was made of brown wood. On the top was a small round window from where you could first have a look at all the visitors. In the middle there was a shiny brass knocker.

A door like so many others in the apartment buildings of Vienna.

We step over the thresholds of our homes countless times and only rarely do we remember doing so.

I was eleven years old and stood on the other side of the door.

A last kiss and my father freed himself from my hug. With an old schoolbag under his arm, as if he would be gone for just a few hours, he turned toward the door. A last goodbye and he was on his way to the train station.

Everything as usual—only this time he tried to cross over the Belgian border.

Kristallnacht had already passed.

Four years later my mother and I left as well.

My mother didn't lock the door. Why bother?

She looked at the closed door and leaned up against it as if she had become suddenly weak. With tears in her eyes she slid her hand over the brown wood.

Then she picked up the bags off the floor and we went on our way to the rallying point. From there we were supposed to be transported to the Theresienstadt Ghetto.

Now the war had come to an end and I returned as fast as possible to Vienna. I was one of the first to return from the camps.

My hand approached the doorbell. Who would open the door? Would it be someone I didn't know; would I have to first explain who I was? It took all the courage I had to ring the doorbell.

I could see an eye through the peephole. Then the door opened just a bit, just as far as the safety chain would reach.

An older woman stood there. She used to be the cleaning lady and she had known my mother from childhood. As I remembered, she had been an inseparable part of the household. She regarded the figure in front of her with an overtly astonished look—thin, half boy, half girl, short stubble covering its scalp. Then she puffed out, "Wow, Miss Eva…you're still alive too?!"

She let me in, but as I crossed the threshold I knew that for me it wasn't the same anymore.

Chapter 13:

Relatives

Vienna, June of 1945; in the morning.

Only one man still stood in front of me at the booth. I discovered a place where they kept a list of names of camp survivors.

I was still hoping.

But when it was my turn I was told no, nobody from my family appeared on the list. And that's how I left with one more disappointment in my heart

Nevertheless I left my name in case anyone should ask for me.

It was lunchtime and as usual I was on my way to the soup kitchen of the Jewish community.

Some young people were already sitting around a few big tables. They had returned, like me, from the concentration camps or came out of their hiding places.

The menu was different every day: beans, lentils, peas, barley, and then it started over.

Vienna hungers.

Every Sunday adventurous people with backpacks got on the train to travel to Vienna's beautiful surroundings. They spread out in the valleys and picked as much fruit from the heavily loaded trees as they could. The owners didn't care: They would have just let the fruit go bad on the trees. Why all the work? Money was worthless anyway.

A small number of people bartered with the farmers—a piece of material for butter, flints for potatoes.

One day I received a letter. My mother's cousin, who was half Jewish, had never left Vienna all these years, and invited me to come visit her.

I sat in her small apartment and looked at the picture of the soldier that was hanging over the bed. Toni had fallen during the war. She was allowed to take his name even though they had only been engaged.

She got ahold of her father's diary from the Theresienstadt Ghetto. Everything was written down in it—when my mother and I were transported to Auschwitz and also how my stepfather with his little daughter went the same way.

A handicapped man and a twelve-year-old child—hopeless to try to wait for their return.

The next morning my cousin picked out some underwear from her drawers; then she made plans for our next get-together, which I didn't plan to keep.

Not much later, her younger sister invited me for lunch.

It was a beautiful day and I decided to walk through the city park. I passed the monuments from the city's favorites, Strauss and Lanner, and I sat on a bench in the sun.

The park was full of girls and young women all dressed in their best clothes, which they still owned after six years of war. American soldiers, blacks and whites, mingled with them.

Here nothing was hidden. The soldiers offered cigarettes and chocolate and the girls left with them arm-in-arm.

Marianne's apartment was in the center of the city.

Her old nanny, who had stayed with her all these years, opened the door. I found a spacious apartment, a pretty woman, and a small child.

"That's Peter's son," said Marianne. "Surely you remember our wedding. He had already been drafted. But I divorced him."

On a small table by the wall there were a lot of different kinds of bottles of alcohol, one for every taste.

We sat down at the dinner table. The old nanny served us a good meal with pretty dishes. It was like a meal from a different world.

Between the courses I asked Marianne if she still had our silverware.

I remembered the day exactly when I accompanied my mother to bring it to her in secret. The dark colored boxes in which knives, spoons, and forks rested on shiny blue silk or red velvet. We only stayed a few minutes in the then-modest apartment and left trying not to be seen so we would put Marianne in danger.

First Marianne completely denied it. Finally she admitted that my mother had given her a set of silverware, but it had been a gift.

The doorbell rang. The old nanny announced the arrival of the officer and when she left the room she took the child with her.

A not-so-young colonel entered. His arms were loaded with all kinds of goodies: a Hungarian Salami was clamped between bottles of vodka and red smoked meat peeked through brown wrapping paper.

After he handed all the treasures over to Marianne, she introduced me: “My friend Sascha,” she said, “from the command post.”

I felt like I was a third wheel and said goodbye as soon as possible. Marianne looked at me as if she were trying to read an answer to a question no one had asked.

No, no need to worry. I'm not planning on coming back with helpers to perform a thorough search of the house. I won't return at all.

On the street most of the shops were already closed. They didn't have anything left to sell and for the ones that did still have some merchandise, they found other uses for it.

Some shops weren't reopened after the Jewish owners had been forced to shut them down. The signs still showed the familiar names.

I had passed by here many times with my mother, forcefully pulling her away from the display window only so she could stand in front of the next one.

At this early afternoon hour the street was almost empty.

Why was I going faster—was someone following me?

No, no one. Only shadows followed me, shadows surfacing from my past.

I arrived at the apartment.

There I sat on the sofa trying to figure out a good reason to continue living.

Chapter 14:

The Meeting

People stood in front of the theater entrance. Colorful posters announced the famous Russian ballet. Only the façade of the Vienna State Opera remained; that's why the performance would take place in another theater.

I got in line. I wanted to catch up on everything I had missed for the past few years—to sit in the magnificent hall, to get comfortable in my upholstered chair, and to feel the special expectation before the curtains were pulled back.

All that was new for me. Only once or twice had I gone to the theater with my mother to see a children's performance before the doors were shut for Jews.

The line moved slowly.

In the entry hall near the ticket counter I discovered her. "Dita!" I yelled. She turned around and looked with astonishment at the people behind her. I waved at her with my hand and we met halfway.

Dita and I had lived in the same room when we were in Theresienstadt.

Her mother was here as well.

The two of them saw in Auschwitz how families were forced apart. So they each went their way separately as if they didn't know each other. That's how they were able to live through the terror and hardship until the day of liberation.

That evening in the theater during the intermission, Dita and her mother told me that they had planned to leave Vienna as soon as possible—probably as soon as this coming Sunday. They wanted to cross over the boarder to Pressburg. This was possible with help from the military cars from the Russian troops.

I had just enough time to write down their phone number and address before the lights went out. On stage there were colored costumes, the lights changed continuously, and the sound of the music rushed past my ears. I didn't feel at home; it was as if I didn't belong here.

The curtains closed and the prima ballerina bowed for the last time.

I wished Dita and her mother a good trip, said goodbye, and returned home. "Home." When I returned to Vienna I found two couples, "mixed marriages," in our apartment. They were only willing to give me the middle room to use.

When my family had lived there, that room was the living room.

There was no closet, but for the few things I had the cupboard was sufficient.

In the middle of the room there was a big dining room table. It was surrounded by tall chairs that were in the way of anyone trying to come through from any of the three adjacent rooms. It was just a room for passing through.

I turned the lights off and felt my way to the sofa. I quickly fell asleep, before the nightly procession of the flashlights began.

The next morning my roommates greeted me as always with the same stories about the dripping faucet and the clogged toilet.

I had to get out of this apartment and out of this city where I couldn't bear the inhabitants any longer.

I looked for the note with the telephone number. They were home and I hurried to their apartment.

Yes, I was able to tag along.

We decided on a meeting point.

On Sunday at nine o'clock Dita, her mother, and I stood on the country road that led from Vienna toward the east.

Only Russian military cars passed by here. A few of them stopped, but they didn't have enough room for the three of us. After we decided not to split up we let them go.

It was already past lunchtime and we were still standing on the same street.

We were just contemplating going back when the driver of a military car offered to take us along.

There were a few soldiers on the wooden benches. It didn't take a long explanation—they knew where we wanted to go.

Near the Czech boarder they instructed us to crawl under the benches. For safety's sake, they covered us up with a strip of canvas.

Boarder control stopped the car and through a small hole I saw a head looking over the side wall.

I held my breath, but it was not necessary. The soldiers yelled a few words at them and the truck rolled on.

Calmed, I sat back on the bench. Vienna—never again.

Chapter 15:

A Girlfriend

I rang the doorbell and as the door opened she stood before me. She looked at me and smiled, full of joy.

"Evitschka!" she yelled and I hugged her.

Instantly I understood that "home" was not a specific place, but rather people who loved you. Only now I had returned "home," here in a strange city where I had never been before. I had come to Lisa seeking asylum; she wouldn't disappoint me.

"I would like to stay here in Prague," I whispered.

"That's fine," she said. She added, "You know, Jackie has returned."

She told me about her upcoming wedding. They had waited for years. They had already been a couple during the youth movement.

Lisa's parents and her brother immigrated to Palestine and Jackie and Lisa stayed in Czechoslovakia—just like the movement leader had required them to do.

They came together to the Theresienstadt Ghetto. Lisa was my leader there in the youth quarters. Auschwitz split the two of them apart. But now in the summer of 1945, here in Prague, they had found each other again.

With Lisa's help I moved into the Jewish orphanage.

She even got me a Czech ID. For that purpose a different girl, one who didn't have any language problems, went to the relevant public offices.

I wanted to go to Palestine, but the gates of the country were locked. Visas were only rarely issued. That's why I went to the employment agency. That's where I received an ID with the eagle and the swastika emblazoned on it; not enough time had passed for a new edition.

At a dentist's office I received a small salary, like all other apprentices before me. I had a whole month to think about how I should spend the few crowns.

I was often sent to different quarters to deliver finished work. It was always in the afternoon. Usually I reached the right address quickly, but something happened on the way back; I was captivated by the magically illuminated shop windows.

I didn't buy anything as almost everything was rationed, and I didn't have any money anyway. So I strolled through the streets until all of a sudden I remembered that I needed to return to work.

In the lab they looked at me with raised eyebrows and an astonished "How could you…?"

Soon after the busy Christmas season was over, my employer found an excuse to let me go.

Now window shopping was just about the only thing that kept me busy.

It was around this time that Jackie became ill. They suspected typhoid.

The hospital was outside the city. I drove there with Lisa. Because of the risk of infection there was a big glass wall between the sick patients and the visitors.

Weeks passed without any sign of improvement. Only then did the doctors finally change their diagnosis.

When I returned the glass wall had been removed. They had transported Jackie to the internal medicine unit. He had lost a lot of weight, but his heartbreaking, mischievous smile still appeared from time to time.

In the meantime I became more and more tense. I was afraid that the authorities would uncover the truth and send me back to Vienna. I had to prevent that!

Lisa promised me that she would do everything to help me immigrate to Palestine as soon as possible. I would be getting a certificate for youth immigration.

But time passed and I remained in Prague.

One day I decided to explain to Lisa that the uncertainty was driving me up the wall. I went to her.

Already on the brink of losing it, I poured out all my impatience to her in one breath. She was silent for a moment and then said, "Good that you are here...I almost thought that they had come to announce that Jackie was dead."

I have never been so ashamed as in that moment.

The doctors decided to operate on Jackie. After that they didn't leave her any hope. It was only a matter of time now.

I went to the hospital with Lisa.

His head looked like a skull covered only with skin. His eyes were sunk down deep into the sockets and his nose protruded sharply. His fingers reminded me of the legs of a spider crawling across the covers.

I put a pot with a white hyacinth next to him on the table. He smiled for a brief moment as if to say thank you.

In the spring after Jackie's death we immigrated, Lisa and me together, to Palestine.

The train took us to Paris.

In the spring of 1946 there hadn't been enough time for Paris to recover from the war. Due to a shortage of silk stockings the women in Paris stained their legs with a brown dye. The elevator in the Eifel Tower didn't work.

But the entrances to the Louvre were open. I felt the dimensions of time there—everything passes. Would we be turning into just an "era at some point?

I traversed by metro through Paris. Each time for my next destination I checked the big city map found at every station. That's how I also ended up at Place de la Bastille. I recognized a little late that the only thing that remained from the famous historical place was a memorial plaque.

Three days later we continued to Marseille. In a camp outside the city we spent a week with nothing to do.

Finally the small steam ship named *Cairo* set sail.

In the evening hours one of the immigrants played the accordion; his name was Juda. I begged him to play "Eine kleine Nachtmusik" by Mozart—I used to play it on the violin.

He came from Holland and told me how he survived the war in a closet where his friends had hidden him. They couldn't save his parents.

One morning Lisa called me to come up to the deck. You could see Mount Carmel on the horizon. Slowly the mountain got closer until we could clearly distinguish every house.

The ship cruised into the harbor.

We got off and walked through a dust cloud of disinfectant.

Outside the harbor Lisa's parents and brother were waiting for her. There was also a row of buses.

When the first one filled up, it took me to the immigration camp.

Chapter 16:

You Don't Know Them

No, you don't know them,
The starving,
The bald,
Dressed in rags.
But I myself—
Was one of them.

No, you are not afraid
Of barbed wire,
Electrically charged
All around the fence.
But my girlfriend—
Touched them.

No, you don't remember
The flames,
That rose to the sky
Nightly from the chimneys.
But my mother—
Was burned there!

Yes, you are right:
Hunger, rags,
Barbed wire and chimney—
All that was in the past.

But from deep inside
A scream will echo forever.

Made in the USA
Monee, IL
03 November 2020

46566310R00046